Sylvia Earle

Deep Sea Explorer and Ocean Activist

Women Hall of Famers in
Mathematics and Science

Sylvia Earle

Deep Sea Explorer and
Ocean Activist

Katherine White

the rosen publishing group's
rosen
central

Published in 2004 by The Rosen Publishing Group, Inc.
29 East 21st Street, New York, NY 10010

First Edition

Library of Congress Cataloging-in-Publication Data

White, Katherine, 1975–
  Sylvia Earle : deep sea explorer and ocean activist / by
Katherine White. — 1st ed.
    p. cm. — (Women hall of famers in mathematics and science)
Summary: Examines the personal life and professional career
of Sylvia Earle, who is an oceanographer, marine botanist,
ecological activist, aquanaut, and author.
Includes bibliographical references (p.   ).
ISBN 0-8239-3879-4 (library binding)
1. Earle, Sylvia A., 1935– —Juvenile literature. 2. Marine
biologists—United States—Juvenile literature. 3. Women marine
biologists—United States—Juvenile literature. [1. Earle, Sylvia
A., 1935– . 2. Marine biologists. 3. Scientists. 4. Underwater
exploration. 5. Women—Biography.] I. Title. II. Series.
QH91.3.E2W58 2002
578.77′092—dc21

                                        2002009413

Manufactured in the United States of America

Contents

Introduction

At the age of three, Sylvia Earle fell in love with the ocean when her small body was toppled by a wave. Since then, her relationship with the ocean has swelled, much as ocean waves themselves. Sylvia wrote in her book *Sea Change*, "The 'urge to submerge' came on early and continues, seasoned and made more alluring by thousands of underwater hours, each one heightening the excitement of the last as one discovery leads to another, each new scrap of information triggering awareness of dozens of new unknowns."

She may talk of the ocean as a poet, but Sylvia Earle studies the sea as a scientist. She holds twelve honorary degrees from various colleges and universities, including Duke University and Harvard University. She has spent an astounding 6,000 hours under water, studying marine life, such as fish and plants. She was named the first Hero for the Planet by *Time* magazine in 1998. Sylvia has also written a variety of books on oceans and sea life for both children and adults. She has been published in more than 200 professional journals and magazines, on topics ranging from ecology to ocean life.

Perhaps it is obvious why Sylvia Earle has achieved greatness in her field: She has a supreme level of expertise and knowledge about aquatic life. Sylvia's nicknames—"Her Deepness" and "Queen of the Deep"—echo the respect that the media and her fellow scientists feel for her. Yet all has not come so easily for Sylvia. She has worked exceptionally hard to achieve this level of greatness.

Sylvia's career began in the early 1960s, a time when women's rights were only beginning to be taken seriously. Women such as Gloria Steinem and Betty Friedan were working hard to change the popular ideas of a woman's role in society. They sought to prove that women could be more than just housewives. The women's liberation movement was changing America's social structure. Sylvia Earle, in pursuit of her own dreams, helped to pave the way for change by becoming a marine botanist. She was the first woman to serve as the chief scientist of the National Oceanic and Atmospheric Administration (NOAA). She was one of the first divers to use scuba (self-contained underwater breathing apparatus) gear. And in 1970, Sylvia led a team of aquanauts—divers who visit the ocean, much as astronauts visit space—to live in an underwater chamber for fourteen days as part of the United States government–sponsored Tektite Project.

The above is only a glimpse into the life of an amazing oceanographer, marine botanist, ecologist, aquanaut, and writer. Her life and her accomplishments are a tale of their own, as are her many expeditions to the bottom of the sea. Like the ocean, Sylvia Earle's life has a great many wonders to explore.

Falling in Love with Nature

By 1935, the American stock market had already crashed, and the Great Depression was in full swing. Franklin Delano Roosevelt was two years into his term as the thirty-second president of the United States. Americans were first starting to enjoy listening to the radio and reading mystery novels. On August 30, 1935, in the middle of all of this, Sylvia Alice Earle was born in Gibbstown, New Jersey.

Sylvia's parents, Alice and Lewis Earle, were thrilled with the birth of their second child. Both Alice and Lewis were happy people. They both had an appreciation for life and many original ideas to share with their children. In 1938, when Sylvia was three years old, the family decided to make a move. The Earles moved only a few towns away to Paulsboro, New Jersey.

The family's new farmhouse was not too comfortable when they first moved in. In fact, it was quite run down. There was no water or electricity, and there were more than a few scattered holes in the roof. Sylvia's father worked night and day to fix it up. Although the farmhouse was not in perfect shape, it did have lots of land surrounding it. Both of Sylvia's parents had grown up on farms, and they wanted their children to experience the same diversions and surprises of farm life, which is exactly what Sylvia did in the early years of her life. Each day was a new adventure. She had acres of farmland to explore. She discovered old apple orchards, fields of grapevines, and acres of woods. She even had a pond and a creek to examine.

THE INVESTIGATIONS BEGIN

Sylvia showed enthusiasm for science at a very young age. One of her favorite pastimes was

Sylvia's research began early in life when she investigated her family's pond. Her interest in science and the sea continued when she learned how to scuba dive at age seventeen.

investigating the family's pond. She filled a notebook with descriptions of the pond. What really grabbed Sylvia's attention were all of the little creatures that lived in the pond. She loved the plants and animals that she found in and around the water.

Sylvia would sit as quiet and still as she could, so she would not disturb the pond's natural activity. This is how she would sit for hours, filling her notebooks with facts on the animals' behavior and eating patterns. When she got tired of taking notes, Sylvia would channel her more artistic side. She would draw the creatures scurrying, hopping, and swimming. Soon, Sylvia's investigations evolved, or grew. She began to collect specimens—items used for research and testing in experiments. She gathered various plants that blossomed and budded around the pond. She captured insects, salamanders, and tadpoles and brought them home as pets. Just as she did at the pond, Sylvia would write about how these little animals lived their lives—noting what they ate, when they slept, and what kind of environment they liked the best. Within a short time, the Earle house became Sylvia's first laboratory. Rooms filled up with her collections and research. She had jars everywhere!

Sylvia's parents did not mind. In fact, Sylvia's mother, Alice, encouraged her creativity and interest in animals. Alice also loved animals and nature, and she was glad that her daughter shared her interests. Often, mother and daughter spent afternoons walking together, looking at brightly colored birds while Sylvia collected her beloved plants. In fact, Sylvia's mother was so in love with animals, she was nicknamed the Bird Lady by many of the Earle family's neighbors. She was often seen nursing sick birds back to health, or walking on their farmland, which was filled with tomato plants and huge beautiful gardens, followed close behind by a family of ducks.

Sylvia had many things to explore on her family's farm. The farmland sprouted apples, pears, and walnuts from the hundreds of trees that her father had planted. The Earle farm also harvested corn, asparagus, tomatoes, green peppers, and lima beans. Even though the Earles did not raise animals, Sylvia did have two horses that she loved more than anything. She had a pony named Minnehaha and a quarter horse named Tony. Both horses were very good friends, and Sylvia loved riding around the farm, looking at all the wildlife.

MEETING THE OCEAN

New Jersey sits along the eastern coastline of the United States, making beach trips a pretty popular pastime. Each year, the Earle family would travel to Ocean City, New Jersey—a favorite vacation spot for many people, even now.

In her book *Sea Change*, Sylvia shares her very first experience with the ocean: ". . . a monstrous wall of green water races my way, hissing, roaring, towering, inescapable, sweeping me into a cascading aquatic mayhem. I am lifted, tumbled, churned, pushed, and fall, gasping, clawing for air. My toes touch sand; a sweet breeze soothes my lungs. I stand choking, face the next advancing wall, and leap into it, exhilarated!"

This is the moment Sylvia Earle fell in love with the ocean. She was only three years old, and still she carries this memory with her as the very beginning of her deep aquatic love.

Until 1948, Sylvia vacationed in New Jersey. She spent days swimming in the ocean, crabbing along the docks, and collecting seashells. When she was at home, she collected her plants and animals as she explored during the mornings and afternoons, only to study her great finds in the evening. Perhaps you can see the ingredients of a

Sylvia (right) *fell in love with the ocean at a very young age, when she collected aquatic specimens on her family's property. Here, Sylvia poses under water for a picture while collecting samples of plants.*

future scientist—an instantaneous love for the ocean and a passion to research anything, even things in her own backyard.

MOVING RIGHT BESIDE THE SEA

One would think that a twelve-year-old who loved the ocean would be excited to move right beside it. But Sylvia was less than thrilled when the Earles decided to relocate to Florida.

In 1948, things were not going so well for Sylvia's dad, Lewis, at the factory where he worked. Lewis's job was not as fulfilling as he would have liked, and, after talking with his brother in Florida, he thought starting an electrical contracting business down there might be a change for the better. On top of this, Sylvia's younger brother, Evan, was pretty sick. Both factors caused Sylvia's parents to take action. They believed warmer weather would be good for Evan's health, and they also thought that starting a business would be a great opportunity. Sylvia, however, was hesitant about such a big change. She loved the land surrounding her family's farm, and she was sad to say good-bye. The land, her adventures, and her plant collecting were ending. Thankfully, Sylvia's mood turned around when she got her first glimpse of the Gulf of Mexico.

The town of Dunedin is only a few minutes outside of Clearwater on the western side of Florida. The Gulf of Mexico was Sylvia's new backyard! She was exhilarated. Not only was the water so clear she could see the bottom, but it also revealed all the little plants and animals scurrying along the ocean floor. The water was so different from the grayer, murkier water of New Jersey's shore. Now, Sylvia could spend every day in the ocean. She would never run out of things to explore.

A LOVE FOR LEARNING

When Sylvia entered school in New Jersey, her teachers noticed her love for science. After moving to Florida and starting at a new school, Sylvia's teachers once again picked up on her deep interest in the sea. All of them worked to help Sylvia learn as much as she could about the ocean and marine animals. Sylvia could not get enough of underwater exploration. So, like many young people who love a certain subject, she turned to books. She read everything she could about deepwater explorers such as Jacques Cousteau and William Beebe. Each adventure she read about spurred more interest and made Sylvia realize one thing: She needed to become a great swimmer.

WILLIAM BEEBE: UNDERWATER ADVENTURER

William Beebe was born on July 29, 1877, in Brooklyn, New York. Like Sylvia, Beebe fell in love with science and nature at a young age. He decided to build a career out of exploring oceans and studying animals.

Beebe's interest in oceans took him to many places, such as Mexico, Asia, the Galapagos Islands, and the jungles of South America. He wrote books on almost all of his adventures. Some of these

Continued on Page 20

William Beebe (right) *and Otis Barton pose for a picture with the bathysphere.*

Continued from Page 19

books include *Galapagos, World's End,* and *Beneath Tropic Seas.*

On August 15, 1934, after a series of dives, Beebe and his partner, Otis Barton, made their record-breaking descent of 3,028 feet (about 923 meters) under water. In that instance, the sea craft, called the bathysphere, withstood more than 1,360 pounds of pressure—an amazing accomplishment. They held the record for the deepest dive for fifty-two years!

FISH OUT OF WATER

In *Sea Change,* Sylvia shares how her older brother, Lewis, had the most elegant freestyle crawl. While growing up, she often felt a twinge of envy as she watched him cut cleanly through the water. Even though Sylvia could not master the freestyle stroke, she had a gift for swimming under water. She just knew exactly what to do to propel herself forward and glide smoothly. This was her gift, and she used it over and over again throughout her life. Learning to swim would be the beginning of Sylvia's travels under water.

2

Underwater Exploration Begins

Throughout the 1990s, scuba-diving equipment made some major advances. These improvements and developments greatly improved the scuba diver's underwater experience. Divers could breathe easier, stay under water for longer periods of time, and go deeper into the depths of the sea. One of the biggest innovations was the mixing of gases, such as oxygen and helium, to make air for the diver to breathe. Scientists had been experimenting with different amounts of gases for years. After many attempts, they finally were able to successfully recreate the air that we breathe for divers to breathe below the surface of the water. Full

In the 1950s, scuba-diving technology was advancing. Special equipment helped divers to breathe easier under water, making diving a much more pleasant experience.

face masks, underwater voice communication, and computer systems also brought diving to a great new level. You can probably imagine then that forty years before in the 1950s, diving technology was not nearly as advanced.

DIVING IN

At sixteen years old, Sylvia had her first dive. A friend's father owned diving equipment and invited her along for a dip in the Weeki Wachee River in Florida. Keep in mind that this was 1951. Scuba technology was very different than it is today. Sylvia had to wear a heavy helmet that filled up with air and pushed hard on her bare shoulders. The air in the helmet hurt her ears and the suit made it difficult for her to walk through the water. She also had to be attached to a hose while under water—the hose pumped air to her helmet so that she could breathe. Yet Sylvia, always the optimist and adventurer, pushed her discomfort aside and concentrated on the amazing experience she was about to have.

When her feet touched bottom, she was exhilarated. She looked around and met the flashing eyes of an alligator! She watched as the huge animal opened and closed its mouth a few times. She saw the gator's sharp teeth. Fascinated and enthralled, she stepped toward the animal just as it swished and flicked it's strong tail. This movement created such a rush of current that she was almost knocked over. She proceeded on,

Sylvia (left) *had her first dive when she was only sixteen years old. Here, in 1997, she and an unidentified diver attempt to document the fish population on a two-week program called the Great American Fish Count.*

moving from the middle of the river to the side of the stream. A school of small, gold-brown fish swam around the edge. She walked toward them with bubbles rising all around her. They turned and headed toward her, then swam all around her. Sylvia was amazed! She felt as if she were a part of the river.

Suddenly though, Sylvia felt a wave of dizziness. It felt strange and uncomfortable. She tugged the hose—a sign for wanting to come up—just as someone dived down and pointed for her to return to the boat as quickly as possible. When she was safely out of the water and inside the boat, her friends told her that exhaust fumes from the air generator were getting into the hose and sending her a deadly mix of carbon dioxide, carbon monoxide, and a few other toxic gases. Sylvia was lucky that she was not hurt. As Sylvia relates in *Sea Change*, she learned a very big lesson that day: Never take clean air for granted, both above the water and beneath it.

LEARNING HER TRADE

Sylvia's first dive did not quench her love for exploration for very long. Instead, it turned her thoughts to how soon she could go down again. She had a taste for water exploration and she was consumed with when and how she would get to plunge beneath the water's surface and explore the worlds below once again. When she was seventeen, she figured out how she could get more diving experience: She went to college.

During the summer of 1952, when she was only seventeen years old, Sylvia signed up for a marine biology class at Florida State University. She had yet to even graduate from high school but her knowledge of science and nature extended very far beyond the average high school student.

Harold Humm was the marine biology professor for Sylvia's class. His belief was that a student learns more from hands-on experience than from sitting in the classroom. Most of the class time was geared to diving expeditions. In 1952, there were no laws as there are now requiring divers to be officially certified. This meant all of the students could take their plunge into the water without much preparation.

The class's first dive was off the shore of St. Mark's Wildlife Refuge in Florida. Harold gave Sylvia two words of advice when she was about to head down into the water: "Breathe naturally." If Sylvia did not breathe naturally, she would experience something called the bends. The medical term for the bends is decompression sickness. It is a very real hazard for divers though it does not happen that often if a diver is careful and well trained.

Basically, the bends occurs for one reason: The longer a diver stays down and the deeper a diver goes, the more nitrogen dissolves in the tissue of the diver's body. If the diver comes up, or ascends, too rapidly the dissolved nitrogen comes out too quickly and forms bubbles in the body's tissues. The diver could experience severe pain, dizziness, blindness, paralysis, or convulsions. This was just one of the things Sylvia was to learn during her first few dives.

JACQUES YVES COUSTEAU: MAN OF THE SEA

Jacques Cousteau devoted his entire life to sea exploration. He was serving in the French navy when he realized his love for ocean exploration, and only a few years later he was known around the world for it. One of Cousteau's greatest accomplishments came in 1943, when he and French engineer Emile Gagnan perfected the aqualung—a cylinder of compressed air that attached to a face mask, allowing divers to stay under water for hours.

Though he was accomplished as an explorer, Cousteau was just as enthusiastic about sharing his love of the sea with others. His best-known series of books, *Undersea Discoveries of Jacques Yves Cousteau,* was one of Sylvia's favorite reads as a child. She bought every book that came out in the series and read them all more than a few times. She loved the way Cousteau made the ocean come alive on the page. One of Sylvia's favorite movies, *Silent World*, was also done by Jacques Cousteau. Even now, Sylvia still calls Cousteau one of her biggest role models. When Cousteau passed away in 1997, Sylvia knew the world had lost one of the greatest ocean explorers of all time.

A PERFECT DIVE

Sylvia's first dive in her college marine biology class took place where the water's depth reached only 15 feet (about 4.6 meters). This allowed the diver to reach the ocean floor quickly, and in case of an emergency, return to the surface just as fast. When Sylvia touched bottom on a mass of soft, brown seaweed, she became elated and immediately glided over to a bouquet of sponges where she spotted a type of fish called a damselfish. Sylvia had seen this type of fish before during breath-holding dives, but she could stay down longer this time. Staying longer under water allowed the fish time to become comfortable with her presence and she was able to watch as the fish returned to their normal state.

When Sylvia returned to the surface, she was bursting with enthusiasm. Each dive created this feeling for her, and with only a few diving experiences under her belt, Sylvia began to formulate a life plan.

MAKING PLANS FOR THE FUTURE

During the 1950s, women did not have many choices when it came to their careers. It was not like it is today, where a young woman can be anything she wants to be. Sylvia was raised during a time when society was less open-minded. Yet Sylvia did not want to be an English teacher or a nurse, which is what most women became at that time. Sylvia loved the ocean too much. She decided to go to college to become a marine biology professor. She wanted to share her passion for the ocean with her students.

This was a big decision for a seventeen-year-old during the 1950s. Such a bold move was not expected of women. But Sylvia knew what she wanted, and she was determined to achieve her goals. Little did she know exactly how much she would impact those she taught and the world in general.

3

A Career Under Water

The transition from high school to college is challenging for every young person who chooses this path. Important decisions have to be made, and much thought needs to be invested in these decisions. After graduating high school, Sylvia decided to spend a year at St. Petersburg Junior College—she was close to home and her transition into college life was made smoother by this decision. However, the following year she was ready for a bigger change, so Sylvia transferred to Florida State University in Tallahassee. The school offered her close to a full scholarship.

BACHELOR'S DEGREE AND BEYOND

Harold Humm, Sylvia's first college professor, also played a big part in her transfer. Sylvia had kept in contact with Harold and he inspired her to move on to Florida State University. Still a professor there, Harold took Sylvia under his wing. He saw so much potential and passion in her. He supported her interest in the ocean by teaching her as much as he could. The two forged a great friendship because they both shared a deep love for learning as well as a true love for the sea. Sylvia also spent a lot of time at the science laboratory because she worked there for extra money.

Sylvia studied exceptionally hard during her four years at Florida State. She was enthusiastic about learning, and she dedicated herself to absorbing as much knowledge as she could. In 1955, she received her bachelor's degree in marine botany. Few people who knew her were surprised that she wanted to go to the next level and continue learning about the ocean.

Sylvia was accepted into the master's degree programs at Yale University, Cornell University, and Duke University. Sylvia chose Duke University in North Carolina for two reasons. First, they offered her a full scholarship, meaning they paid for her tuition, books, and room and board. However, she also picked Duke for a more personal reason. Going there would allow her to work with Harold Humm once again. Professor Humm had moved from Florida State, and Sylvia wanted another chance to learn from him because she loved the way he taught.

EARNING HER MASTER'S

In 1956, Sylvia earned her master's degree. This huge accomplishment illustrates the immense dedication that Sylvia had toward her career. She studied algae to earn her master's degree, doing experiments on how it thrives in the ocean. During her college years, Sylvia was evolving and changing, as were her goals for the future. She realized that she simply did not want to become a professor anymore. She wanted to work directly with the ocean, a career comprised of studying the sea. She wanted to become a marine biologist and explore the ocean as Jacques Cousteau did. Sylvia knew the hardships that awaited her as a woman trying to become a scientist. But she was up for a challenge.

EARNING RESPECT

At Duke, the students in Sylvia's science classes were mostly men. She was passed up for teaching assistant positions because of her gender. During the course of her education and for years to come, Sylvia struggled against the popular idea that women should be housewives, not scientists. No one had ever told her that she could not become a marine botanist, but she was given less opportunity than her male counterparts. So, how did Sylvia handle this? She worked harder. She did not let other people's ideas get her down. Instead, she concentrated on her own dreams and on achieving them. In

Sea Change, Sylvia shares her feelings about women scientists and the challenge of society's views: "Usually I did not mind being passed over for things that I knew I could do as well or better than men who were being considered, mostly because I understood the reality: No matter how competent a woman is, sometimes society rules that only a man will do. I could play by those rules—or not play."

TWO PIONEER FEMALE SCIENTISTS

Like Sylvia, there have been other women scientists that had met with the idea that women should not have careers in science. The women below are two of the earliest women to fight for a career in the sciences. Undoubtedly, each woman helped to make the path a bit easier for the next generation of women in this field.

Mary Katharine Layne Brandegee (1844–1920)

A physician and botanist, Mary Katharine earned her medical degree from the University of

California in 1874. She was one of the first women to be recognized as a scientist. Two species of plants, the *Astragalus laynea* and the *Mimulus layneae*, are named for her.

Mary E. Pennington (1872–1954)

Mary was refused a degree in chemistry from the University of Pennsylvania when she earned enough credits for her bachelor's degree. Instead, she received a proficiency degree. After two more years of study, she earned her doctorate in chemistry and she went on to become the chief of the Department of Agriculture's food research lab.

Most of the time, Sylvia chose *not* to play by the rules because she wanted more than anything to be a marine botanist.

HER OWN FAMILY

At the age of twenty-one, Sylvia got married. She had met John Taylor, a zoologist, a few years before. After Sylvia was married, she had no intention of

Sylvia has had to juggle many roles in her lifetime. As a scientist, she helped build submarines, such as Deep Rover. Here, Sylvia poses with a robotic arm delicately holding an egg. Part of Sylvia's role as a scientist is to bring science and technology together.

giving up her dreams, so she and John moved back to Dunedin, Florida, into a house right next to Sylvia's parents. She turned her garage into her laboratory and continued to work on her research from the Gulf of Mexico.

In 1960, Sylvia turned her attention to motherhood. She gave birth to her first child, a daughter she named Elizabeth. Just two years later in 1962, Sylvia's second child was born. Baby John, her little boy, helped to complete the family. Sylvia loved being a mother, but she also knew she wanted to accomplish more as a scientist. Many times she had two little people beside her, helping to collect specimens and organize the plants in her laboratory as she took scientific notes. In her book *Sea Change*, Sylvia admits it was very tough at times. She was juggling many roles at once: She was a wife, mother, researcher, and student.

BECOMING A PLANT DOCTOR

A marine botanist's job is to study the plant and animal life in a specific underwater area. The job involves looking for certain aquatic plants (plants

Marine botanists study plant life under water. This giant kelp forest off the coast of California is an example of the exciting and beautiful things that can be discovered in the sea.

that live in and around the ocean) and studying their importance to the environment, fish, and other ocean animals. This means the marine botanist studies the ecology of the ocean. Ecology is the study of the relationship between plants and animals and their environment. After Sylvia earned her master's degree, she began a long-term study on the Gulf of Mexico. She gathered specimens from the water, and then she took them back to her home laboratory, where she would take notes on them. These notes were observations— data collected to learn about a specific topic, in this case marine plants.

Sylvia went back to school again to get her doctorate so that she could become a marine botanist. So, Sylvia was once again attending Duke University to earn that degree. Between her schoolwork and her family, Sylvia had a lot of responsibilities. She was often tired, but she never forgot that her career was incredibly important. In 1964, Sylvia was offered an amazing opportunity, an opportunity that proved her career was blossoming.

A TRIP AROUND THE WORLD

In August 1964, Sylvia was given a huge surprise. The *Anton Bruun*, an old navy ship converted to an exploration vessel for biologists, was about to embark on a journey around the world for six weeks. Sylvia learned of the voyage from a friend who was planning to go. But, at the last second, her scientist friend could not take the trip. Harold Humm, also a passenger, suggested that Sylvia take his place. Even though the voyage was an astounding opportunity to explore water outside of the Gulf of Mexico, Sylvia was more than hesitant—she had two small children to care for at home. She was also still working on her doctorate, and she didn't know if she could take on another time-consuming task.

However, after talking with her husband, her parents, and her school, she found out everyone was 100 percent supportive of her going—this was, after all, the opportunity of a lifetime!

PROVING HERSELF TO AN ALL-MALE CREW

The travel agenda for the trip included many exotic places in and around the Indian Ocean, such as Mombasa, the Amirante Islands, St. Joseph's Reef, the Aldabra group of islands of the Seychelles, Somalia, Dar es Salaam in Tanzania, and Aden in

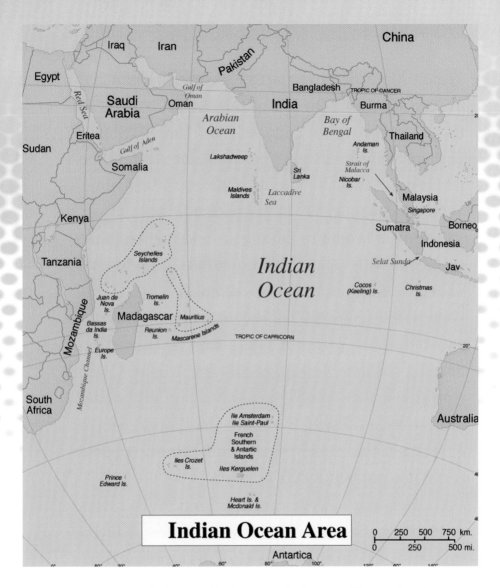

Indian Ocean Area

| 0 | 250 | 500 | 750 km. |
| 0 | | 250 | 500 mi. |

In 1964, Sylvia sailed around the world on the Anton Bruun, *an exploration ship for biologists. She visited areas in and around the Indian Ocean, some of which had not yet been explored by scientists.*

Yemen. Many of these places had yet to be explored by any scientists. On top of this, Sylvia had yet to travel anywhere outside of the United States. Perhaps you can imagine her excitement when she realized she was about to take the trip of a lifetime. Yet a big challenge lay in her path.

Sylvia would be sailing around the world for six weeks with an all-male crew. This brought up a variety of different reactions from the crew members. Some scientists who were going on the trip still believed an old sea tale that a woman on board a ship would bring bad luck. It may sound ridiculous that well-educated scientists would believe such a myth, but more than a few people expressed this belief. Fortunately, these people could not prevent Sylvia from going on the trip.

Her bags were packed, and Sylvia was ready to go. Yet the day she set sail, she realized that a lot of other people had negative feelings toward her being on board with an all-male crew. A newspaper called the *Mombasa Daily Times* ran this headline: "Sylvia Sails Away with 70 Men, But She Expects No Problem." The article ran beside a photo of Sylvia coming out of the water dripping wet.

The article was a big blow to Sylvia, and it caused her to question herself. She went to Harold Humm and expressed her worries. She asked if she was getting in over her head. After all, she had only ever researched the Gulf of Mexico, and she worried that she wouldn't do a good job on the trip. But Harold was an avid supporter of Sylvia. He saw great talent in her work. He reminded her that sometimes people will have different perspectives, but she could not let it affect her work. That conversation shifted Sylvia's own perspective.

ABOARD THE SHIP

Instead of letting negativity get her down, Sylvia used the negative energy as fuel to help her work harder. Her first glimpse of the Indian Ocean also made her realize that she had made the right choice. Sylvia wrote in *Sea Change*, "I focused on the plants, hauntingly similar to those I knew well in the Gulf of Mexico, but with unique ruffles, branches or twists that set them apart. Like a child turned loose in FAO Schwartz, I wanted to be everywhere at once, peering into the great, soft folds of clownish anemones, poking at giant sea cucumbers, following pairs of yellow butterfly fish, standing on my head to get a better look at a spotted eel in an angled crevice, coaxing a tiny octopus from its lair . . ."

During the trip, Sylvia worked extra hard to show her abilities. She often rose at 5 AM and stayed up recording observations until 3 AM. She spent all the time she could in the water, exploring all of the wondrous places below the sea. Sylvia proved her scientific knowledge on that voyage. During the next four years, she went on four more expeditions aboard the *Anton Bruun*.

4

More Nautical Opportunities

In 1965, Sylvia was out on the ocean again, exploring the worlds beneath the sea. She was again aboard the *Anton Bruun*, but this time the ship sailed toward Mas a Tierra, in the Juan Fernandez Islands—a clump of islands a bit west of Chile. This time the scientists were going to explore water that had not been explored scientifically since 1875. All of the scientists aboard the expedition were doing their own research, but they all shared the same goal. Each scientist was full of excitement, because unexplored waters meant opportunities to discover new types of aquatic life.

DISCOVERING A NEW TYPE OF ALGAE

During one of her dives, Sylvia came upon rocks with a mass of thick, pink algae. She had never seen such algae before, so she gathered a specimen before she returned to the surface. Sylvia found out a few days later that she had found a plant that had yet to be discovered!

It was possible that other explorers had seen the pink algae before but had not bothered to classify it. So technically, Sylvia had made her first discovery, and it was her job to name the newly found algae. In science, a plant or animal falls into a nomenclature. Nomenclature is a system used in biology for naming kinds and groups of animals and plants. Nomenclature names are always in Latin.

NAMING HER DISCOVERY

Sylvia was excited about her discovery, but she was also humble. She realized that in the big picture there were millions of ocean plants that had yet to be discovered. She was, however, very excited about the whole experience.

When choosing a name for the algae, Sylvia decided that she wanted to pay tribute to a person who had given her an incredible amount of support and knowledge over the years. After much thinking, Sylvia named the new plant *Hummbrella hydra*. This was her way of saying thank you to her very first college professor and close friend, Harold Humm.

THE SHARK LADY

During one of her many trips aboard the *Anton Bruun*, Sylvia met another female scientist, a rare find back in the 1960s. The two women became fast friends because they shared a lot of the same ideas about science. They also both understood the life of a female scientist because they were both living and experiencing the same difficulties.

Eugenie Clark is known popularly as the Shark Lady. Within the science world, however, Eugenie is an ichthyologist—a person who studies ichthyology. Ichthyology is a branch of zoology that studies fish. Eugenie's favorite fish to study is the shark, and by the time Sylvia met her, Eugenie was known as an expert throughout the world on shark behavior. She too had spent thousands of hours under water studying her passion. She dove with sharks all the time, and she had even established her own laboratory.

On a more personal level, Eugenie had four children, so she and Sylvia would often find comfort and understanding in one another because of the similarities between their careers and families. They often spoke about the challenges of being a scientist, mother, and wife. Eugenie showed Sylvia there was someone else out there who was just as passionate as she was about science, and who also had children at home. In a lot of ways, Eugenie Clark became Sylvia's role model. A role model is a person someone looks up to for their values, accomplishments, and the way he or she lives life.

The two often went diving together and collected samples. In 1965, Eugenie invited Sylvia to work at her laboratory in Sarasota, New York.

Sylvia accepted the offer and happily became the resident director of the lab. While diving on the East Coast, she met with a variety of sharks: lemon, tiger, hammerhead, bull, and, every once in a while, a huge great white shark showed up. Though the experiments and studies were not directly related to Sylvia's plant research, she did learn quite a lot about ecology. She was observing and interacting with one of the ocean's fiercest predators, and she saw how the ocean fit together—how each animal and plant learned to live together as part of a balanced system. She learned about the food chain, and it gave her a broader understanding of oceanic life. Sylvia worked at the laboratory until 1967 while she earned her doctorate at Duke. She completed her doctoral work at the end of 1966.

THE END OF AN ERA

In 1965, Sylvia went through a big change in her personal life. After nine years of marriage to John Taylor, Sylvia and John divorced. The divorce went as smoothly as divorces can. Sylvia and John remained close friends. Sylvia decided to move herself and the children to Boston for a while and commute to Eugenie's laboratory.

Soon after, Sylvia found herself in love again. This time, her love interest was Giles Mead, an ichthyologist. The two got married, and Sylvia gave birth to her daughter, Gale, in 1968. Including Gale, Giles and Sylvia had six children between the both of them. The new household was always packed with enormous amounts of activity. But Sylvia still continued working and diving. In fact, she even dove while she was pregnant with Gale.

MAN-IN-THE-SEA PROJECT

In 1968, Sylvia was invited to participate in a sea exploration in the Bahamas. This time Sylvia would be under water the entire time. How would that happen? She would be on a submarine, the *Sea Diver*, so all of her dives would start out while she was already under the sea. The one catch was that Sylvia was pregnant. Before she said yes to the trip, she sought out many doctors' opinions. Each doctor assured her that the baby would be fine even though Sylvia was a whopping five months into her pregnancy.

Another unique thing about this trip was that Sylvia would be doing all of her "diving" from a dive chamber called *Deep Diver*. The vessel carried two people (actually three with the unborn baby on board). Denny Breese, an expert submariner, and Sylvia were to dive together inside this vessel. The chamber would submerge into the water, then drop Sylvia 125 feet (about 38 meters) deep. The tiny chamber was a unique technology because when it was dropped into the ocean by a crane, the chamber would match the water pressure outside. So, when Denny flung open the hatch door, water did not rush in. It merely sat waiting for Sylvia to slip into the water.

When she emerged from the chamber, Sylvia again felt the rush that she always felt while diving. She walked along the ocean floor, swimming around checking out the scenery. Overall, the dive was a great success! According to Sylvia's daughter, Gale, the dive also inspired a deep love in her for the ocean, too, because she was diving even before she was born!

This experience was like a dream come true for Sylvia. She was able to go deeper into the sea than she ever had before. Little did she know that pretty soon she would be offered an even more amazing chance at sea exploration.

TEKTITE II

In 1969, Sylvia's husband returned home one night to tell her about a flier he had seen while he was at the Smithsonian Institute that day. The flier promoted a new project that was about to get underway. The project was phase II of Project Tektite, a study that invited fifty scientists and engineers to live in an underwater hotel of sorts. Sponsored by the U.S. Navy, the Department of the Interior, and NASA, the project was an incredible opportunity.

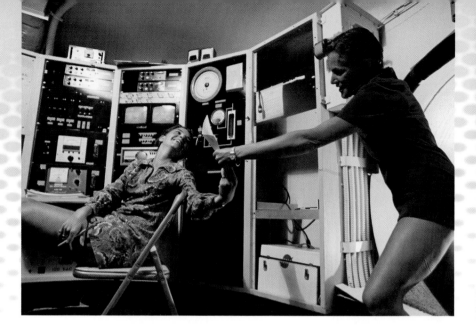

The Tektite II project gave Sylvia (right) *the chance to lead a team of female scientists in an exploration that was well-documented. The underwater research team lived and worked together for two weeks.*

THE HABITAT

The place the scientists would call home for two weeks was rather nice. In fact, a lot of scientists referred to it as the Tektite Hilton, because the interior of the habitat was fully stocked with anything a person would need. A controlled temperature, soft music always playing, a refrigerator, a freezer, a freshwater shower, and comfortable beds were just some of the amenities that the habitat offered. On

Training for the Tektite project began in 1970. Sylvia and the other women scientists researched the effects of pollution and global warming on underwater creatures, as well as the effects that living under water have on the human body.

top of this, the habitat had many portholes, giving it one of the greatest views a scientist could ask for— the ocean lay right outside!

CONTROVERSY

Sylvia was immediately interested in the project because she had been researching how roaming fish (basically, fish in their natural habitat) affect aquatic plants. This project would give Sylvia the perfect opportunity to observe fish during their daily routine. However, she was once again going to experience a challenge because of her gender.

Sylvia describes in *Sea Change* the conversation that she had with Dr. James Miller, the director of the project: "'We didn't expect women to apply' I heard a voice saying . . . I could hear, and almost feel, the embarrassment in his voice, tangible right through the phone line . . ." Sylvia immediately stressed her deep interest and also shared that she was not alone, that other women scientists wanted a chance. The director had actually received other women's applications and their ideas were so good

From inside the Tektite *habitat, the scientists could see all around them. Here, Sylvia* (right) *is diving outside the vessel, communicating with Peggy Lucas, an engineer.*

that the government knew they could not be ignored. Dr. Miller asked Sylvia what she thought about heading an all-female team. Nothing was official yet, but it soon would be.

MISSION 6

Controversy flared when the press found out there was a chance that women and men would be living under water together for two weeks. Only a few days after national newspapers ran the stories, Sylvia was informed that she would head an all-female team! No men would be under water with the women, it was their own project—a major leap forward for women scientists. The team was called Mission 6. They were going to live under water studying plant life for two whole weeks.

Again, though, Sylvia met with frustration when a newspaper article in the *Boston Globe* was run with the headline, "Beacon Hill Housewife to Lead Team of Female Aquanauts." Exactly what frustrated Sylvia about the article? First, Sylvia was not a housewife—she was a mother and a wife. Second, by this time, Sylvia was a rather distinguished scientist, so she was frustrated with the lack of recognition the article paid to her accomplishments. She also kept thinking to herself that when the all-male team headed down to the bottom of the sea, no newspaper would run an article with the headline, "Beacon Hill Husband to Lead Team of Male Aquanauts." Instead, the article would call him a scientist.

GETTING READY FOR TEKTITE

Frustrations left behind, Sylvia approached Tektite with huge waves of enthusiasm. She was ready for the experience, and when the day finally arrived, she was breathless with anticipation.

The all-female team was made up of:

- Dr. Sylvia Earle, director of Mission 6
- Dr. Margaret Lucas, an ocean engineer
- Dr. Renate True, an oceanographer
- Dr. Alina Szmant, an oceanographer
- Dr. Ann Hurley, an oceanographer

Each woman was intensely devoted to her research and the shared goals that they had set for this project. Sylvia was specifically excited because the government supplied the mission with the best underwater equipment available. Sylvia would use a rebreathing system, a new form of underwater technology. The "rebreathing" comes from the fact that the diver carried a small pack on his or her back that recycled breathed air. The system allowed Sylvia to move through the water without making air bubbles—a usual occurrence with scuba gear. Air bubbles often create a disturbance in the natural environment and lead to the fish having different behavior than normal. Without the bubbles, Sylvia could gather fantastic notes on the normal behavior of fish with aquatic plants. She also gathered 124 plant species during the two weeks under water!

Overall, each aquanaut accomplished her goal, and the project was considered an astounding success. Their arrival home mirrored what they felt they had accomplished. They rode in a tickertape parade, and they were invited to lunch at the White House.

5

Success Comes Quickly

After Tektite, Sylvia found herself in a new place within her career. She was suddenly thrust into the life of a recognized and accomplished scientist. Sylvia was now living her dreams. She had earned her doctorate in 1966, and by the start of the 1970s, all of her hard work had finally paid off. She was being considered for a lot of different positions at universities and science labs throughout the world. She was also receiving many invitations to participate in explorations.

Along with scientific recognition, Tektite also caused Sylvia to become a public figure. Suddenly, she found herself in the forefront of the public eye. She was being promoted as an ocean advocate—a person who talks to the public about the importance of a specific subject, trying to raise awareness, motivation, and support. At first, Sylvia had mixed feelings about her new popularity with the public.

SYLVIA'S PUBLIC IMAGE

Sylvia had always kept herself out of the public eye. She was a scientist. Her passion was the ocean and her laboratory. She enjoyed expeditions and exploring far-off places, always thankful she was gaining scientific experience. She never thought about becoming a scientific celebrity, and for a long time, she had mixed feelings about public appearances. After Tektite, though, Sylvia had little choice but to accept the hundreds of public speaking and interview invitations she received. After a few interviews, Sylvia had quite a shift in her attitude toward the media.

Sylvia started to view each interview the same way she viewed her voyages: as an

Sylvia's work forced her to become aware of environmental issues such as pollution and global warming. Here, Sylvia discusses the pollution caused by the Persian Gulf War with William Reilly (left), head of the Environmental Protection Agency. Sylvia's environmental consciousness has taken her to lecture at countless events.

exploration. In 1970, Sylvia appeared on a variety of television shows. She was interviewed by some of the best news personalities of the times, such as Barbara Walters and Hugh Downs. In each interview, she worked hard to shift the lighter questions, like "Did you see any sharks?" to more scientific ones. Sylvia worked to send more important messages about the ocean, such as the need for more exploration and the need for environmental cleanliness. Overall, she found the whole experience challenging and invigorating.

In fact, throughout 1971, Sylvia found herself at speaking engagements and lecture series almost every week. At each event she tried to send a strong message to the public. She stressed the importance of oceans and oceanic life. She talked of the need to keep the oceans healthy as well as the need to keep studying and exploring them. Once again, Sylvia's positive attitude opened doors and paved roads to new opportunity.

NATIONAL GEOGRAPHIC CALLS

In 1971, Sylvia received a call from William Graves, an editor at *National Geographic*. The magazine wanted her to write a story about her experiences during the Tektite project. Sylvia questioned whether or not she wanted to write an article. She realized that as a scientist it was hard to straddle both the scientific world and the public one simultaneously. Often, scientists lost respect for the person who chose "popular science."

On a more personal level, Sylvia also worried about her ability to reach the public. She used such incredibly scientific words when she talked about science that she wondered if she would be able to hold a reader's attention. However, after much thought she decided to write the article, because she thought it was a wonderful opportunity to teach people about the ocean.

OCEAN FACTS

- Ninety percent of all volcanic activity occurs in the oceans.
- The oceans cover 71 percent of Earth's surface and contain 97 percent of Earth's water.
- At the deepest point in the ocean, the pressure is more than eight tons per square inch, or the equivalent of one person trying to support fifty jumbo jets.
- If mined, all the gold suspended in the world's seawater would give each person on Earth nine pounds of gold.

The total length of the world's coastlines is about 313,200 miles (504,000 kilometers), enough to circle the equator twelve times.

Eight percent of all life on Earth is found under the ocean surface.

The first plants on Earth, the algae, developed in the sea 3.5 million years ago.

The average depth of the ocean is 12,450 feet (3,795 meters).

A DANGEROUS MOMENT

Sylvia worked for a long time on her article for *National Geographic*. She chose to write about a potential disaster that occurred during Tektite. In *Sea Change*, Sylvia shares her knowledge about diving. She says that when diving, the biggest danger does not come from sharks, jellyfish, or other creatures in the deep sea. She says that the most fatal mistake a diver can make is to panic.

During one of her Mission 6 dives, Sylvia experienced a moment that could have lead to her death.

She was out swimming and gathering observations when she realized she was out of air. Rather than panic, Sylvia swam toward her diving partner— always a must while diving—and signaled to her partner that she was out of air. Her partner that day was Margaret Lucas, a woman whom everyone called Peggy. When Sylvia gave the sign to Peggy, the other diver reacted calmly. She and Sylvia simply made their way back to the habitat while buddy breathing. Buddy breathing is a standard procedure in diving. It consists of passing a mouthpiece containing air back and forth between divers. Though simple, buddy breathing is very important during a crisis.

That day Sylvia and Peggy arrived back to the habitat perfectly safe, sharing the mouthpiece. A potentially fatal dive was turned around because both Peggy and Sylvia reacted calmly and without panic.

REACHING A NEW AUDIENCE

When Sylvia saw her article published in *National Geographic* in 1971, she was pretty unimpressed with the title. The article was entitled "All Girl Team Tests the Habitat." Sylvia was thirty-four years old. The youngest person on the voyage to the deep sea was twenty-three years old, and all of them were scientists. Sylvia was once again frustrated with the media's lack of respect for women scientists. She realized that *National Geographic* was following the same wave of interest that used the nickname "Aquababes" to describe female scientists. After some thought, Sylvia chose to be positive, so she viewed the article as a chance to reach two million readers and share her love for aquatic life.

A TINY SUBMARINE

By 1975, most underwater labs, like the habitat, had been dismantled. However, one underwater laboratory called *Hydrolab* was still being used. In April 1975, Sylvia was chosen as a team leader for an expedition called SCORE Project. SCORE stands for Scientific Cooperative Operational Research Expedition, and during this exploration,

The Johnson Sea-Link *prepares to dive. Above water you can see clearly the complex mechanics of this submersible. Specialized equipment allows the crew to work from within the vessel, instead of sending divers out into the water.*

Sylvia was going 250 feet (about 76 meters) deep into the ocean in a tiny submarine.

Back in 1970, when the original habitat program began, Ed Link, a scientist, dreamt of a day when divers would be able to explore greater depths. He soon partnered with Seward Johnson,

Under water, the Johnson Sea-Link *illuminates its surroundings. The vessel is equipped with arc lights, which light even the darkest underwater areas. The* Johnson Sea-Link *is equipped with cameras to document its explorations.*

an industrialist and sailor. The two men began work on an underwater vehicle. By 1975, they had perfected the *Johnson Sea-Link I* and *Johnson Sea-Link II* underwater vehicles. The inventions were commonly called bubble subs, because even though they were much smaller than submarines, the vehicles had a large bubble sphere. The sphere was made out of acrylic, and it allowed a driver and a diver to clearly observe the deepest depths in the ocean. However, before Sylvia could plunge in, she had to use a decompression chamber.

LEARNING TO DECOMPRESS

During Tektite, Sylvia and her four team members had to sit in a decompression chamber for twenty-one hours before they could step back on land. What's the reason for this?

Water pressure increases with the depth of the water. When a diver is in very deep water, there is more water above, pressing down on him or her. This pressure can cause a variety of reactions ranging from feelings of intense euphoria to convulsions. None of these extreme feelings are good for a diver's health. Decompression chambers reduce the pressure within the diver's body by changing oxygen and nitrogen levels. The chamber mimics the ocean's depth, easing the diver's body into increased pressure. The whole point is to slow down the process of pressurizing the body—slower speed gives the diver's body time to adjust without any unhealthy side effects.

USING HERSELF TO EXERIMENT

Decompression was usually a lengthy process, and scientists were working on shortening the time a diver had to spend decompressing after a dive. In April 1975, Sylvia emerged from the decompression chamber of the bubble sub, already fifty feet (about fifteen meters) below the ocean's surface. While inside the submarine, her body had already adjusted to the pressure normally felt at fifty feet below the surface. However, on this day Sylvia's reaction to the water was a test in itself. Never before had anyone attempted to decompress in the middle of the ocean—divers always decompressed on land. Sylvia tested a theory that had only been tested before in nonhuman experiments. Her dive proved that a diver experienced less pressure if he or she started out deeper in the water. In other words, decompression chambers could be used for shorter periods of time if the diver plunged into the water at deeper levels. This cut down the time spent in a decompression chamber, making diving far easier.

GETTING TO KNOW THE HUMPBACK

In 1977, Sylvia received another amazing invitation. Katy and Roger Payne, two biologists who focused on whale studies, invited Sylvia and her children along on a trip to the Hawaiian Islands. The couple had been doing research on whales for many years, and they thought Sylvia would enjoy the chance to get to know another creature that lived in the ocean. Sylvia was more than excited about the chance to swim with the huge creatures. The three scientists would be studying the humpback whale.

Some might think that humpback whales are the most interesting fish in the sea. But actually, they're not fish. Humpback whales, like all whales, are warm-blooded animals, meaning they are actually mammals. They have stocky bodies

Humpback whales can stay underwater for about thirty minutes, although their dives usually last about fifteen minutes. In recent years, the humpback whale population has declined dramatically. Sylvia Earle's research helped scientists to understand and protect the whale population.

and flat, broad heads. Full-grown males average forty-two feet (about thirteen meters) in length and weigh about twenty-five tons. The female humpback whale is larger. They average about forty-five feet (about fourteen meters) in length and weigh about thirty-five tons. Grooves run along the underside of humpbacks from their chins to their navels. Both sexes have flippers that are long and winglike with bumps on the front edges. They also have blowholes on the top of their heads to help them breathe when they come to the surface for air.

SWIMMING WITH WHALES

Though Sylvia had a great amount of respect for whales, she was a bit nervous about swimming with them. She was wracked with nervousness as she first got into the water, mainly because she was not used to swimming with such large creatures. Two photographers, Chuck Nicklin and Al Giddings, were out with her to take pictures of their adventure. All three of them were in the water when all of a sudden a pregnant female whale shot up from the ocean's depth. Despite her bulk, the whale moved really quickly. Al Giddings was busy taking pictures, and he did not notice that the whale was heading straight for him. Humpbacks are known to be very gentle mammals, but their size can pose big problems.

The whale's flipper was heading right for Al's head. The photographer was so taken by the moment that he did not even realize what was happening. Sylvia felt a pang of fear turn to relief as the whale's flipper flicked upward and missed his head. Sylvia relaxed and learned to trust the whales, and the rest of the diving went smoothly. She gained enormous amounts of observations and insight into the lives of whales during the three months that she dove with them in and around Hawaii.

When Sylvia returned from her trip to Hawaii, she decided to move her family to Oakland, California, to follow up the project. She was in the process of her second divorce, and she thought the change would be good for her whole family. Though emotionally drained, Sylvia took a few months to regain a balanced life. She worked on her humpback whale observations and spent a lot of time with her children. She relaxed with them, enjoying their active and creative energy.

6

Diving into Her Own Ideas

After relaxing in California for a while, and recuperating from her divorce, Sylvia returned to her active lifestyle. One of her first projects was something entirely new for her. First she would be diving 1,250 feet (381 meters) into the ocean—deeper than she had ever gone before. In fact, the dive was going to be the deepest untethered human dive in history! An untethered dive means Sylvia would not be attached to anything while she dove—no lifelines, no cranes, nothing but her and the deep sea.

A NEW TECHNOLOGY

Al Giddings, the same photographer that Sylvia worked with in Hawaii, came to her and proposed the original idea. He thought it would be a good way to get people excited about ocean exploration again. At that time, a lot of scientists were frustrated with the lack of popularity surrounding ocean exploration. Al and Sylvia were ready to do something about it. They got ABC television and *National Geographic* interested in the project. The television station was going to do a two-hour special on the event and *National Geographic* would do a huge article on it. They were motivated and excited, and they had the technology they needed to complete their mission.

Sylvia would be using a Jim suit to help her reach the deepest depths of the ocean. The concept of the Jim suit, named after diver Jim Jarrett, was originally thought of in 1965 in Britain. However, it took another ten years before the suit became practical and popular. By 1979, when Sylvia began to train to use the suit, the Jim had gone through

Sylvia trained extensively to use the Jim suit, which allowed her to travel to depths that had only previously been explored in submarines. She still holds the record for the world's deepest untethered dive for this amazing feat.

many variations. Phil Nuytten, who owned the patent for the suit—meaning he was the only person at that time who could produce and sell it— hopped aboard the project willingly. He was excited to see how the suit functioned that deep in the water without being connected to a tether.

Learning to use the Jim suit was not an easy task. Sylvia had to be trained to use the complex suit. First, the suit was heavy and very mechanical

Sylvia is lowered into the water to begin her trip 1,250 feet (381 meters) below the surface of the ocean. While under water, she observed many new and exciting sea creatures.

in its design. It was not free moving, and it looked and moved much as a robot would. Sylvia had to learn to walk in the suit and move about in it as well. She worked ferociously at mastering the Jim, and with a few months of preparation and a few test dives, she was ready for the big day.

A HISTORICAL DIVE

On October 19, 1979, Sylvia made her adventure 1,250 feet into the sea. Al Giddings went along to film the whole experience. In *Sea Change*, Sylvia shares this momentous event:

"I landed with the sub in the midst of at least a hundred coral colonies, miraculously managing not to crush any, although several were within easy reach . . . The most gentle nudge of 'my claw' provoked a ring of blue light to pulse . . . Curious, I touched one of the spires at the base and near the tip and watched, anxious to see what would happen . . . Serenely, the miniature fiery blue doughnuts merged, then each passed through the other and continued onward."

Sylvia poses with her husband and business partner, Graham Hawkes. Together, they formed Deep Ocean Technology, a company that builds deep-sea vessels such as the Deep Rover *and* Deep Flight.

Sylvia spent two-and-a-half hours exploring the sea that day. She even planted an American flag on the ocean floor! Although she had enjoyed such a long dive, she was sad that she had to return to the surface. As always, she wanted to stay down there forever to swim about, exploring the sea.

SPARKING NEW INTEREST

By 1981, Sylvia was ready to branch out and work for deep-ocean exploration, but in a different way than she had in the past. She accomplished this by starting her own business, called Deep Ocean Technology. Her business partner was her new husband, Graham Hawkes—they had married in 1980. The primary goal of the company was to build vehicles that helped explorers move through the ocean. The couple ran the business out of their home, and though the company had a bit of a rough start, they hit success in 1984 when they unveiled a major leap in ocean diving technology.

The new ocean vessel, or submersible, was called *Deep Rover*, and it was a one-man sub that could go 3,000 feet (about 914 meters) deep. The sub was a huge leap for divers, because they could drive the vehicle and explore greater depths for longer periods of time.

GOING DOWN, DEEP

In 1985, Sylvia and her husband took *Deep Rover* out for a spin. They each went down separately 3,300 feet (1,006 meters) into the Pacific Ocean, a distance that was unequalled at the time. During Sylvia's second dive in November 1985, she came

In 1984, Deep Ocean Technology unveiled Deep Rover, *which was a big advance in diving technology. Here, Graham Hawkes models the plans for the ocean vessel.*

face to face with a huge surprise. Sylvia was down observing the behavior of dolphins when she spotted a Soviet submarine. At that time in history, the relationship between the United States and the Soviet Union was not very friendly, so when the sub approached *Deep Rover*, Sylvia became nervous. Luckily, all the crew did was wave to Sylvia as they passed by. Sylvia waved back with an uneasy smile and a great sigh of relief.

On land, the Deep Rover's *complexity can be fully appreciated. It is equipped with robotic arms and is designed for maximum comfort of the driver. Since its initial conception, it has been used by many to explore the deep sea.*

Sylvia and Graham's company had a major upswing after *Deep Rover*. They had entered the ocean-vehicle market and their company was gaining recognition. The couple had been working on a new vehicle called *Deep Flight* for many years, and in 1988, they received major funding from IMAX, a film company. In exchange for the use of the vehicle to film under water, the company supplied Deep Ocean Technology with enough money to complete work on this new project. *Deep Flight* was different from *Deep Rover* because it was even easier to handle. It also carried only one person, but the vehicle was much more simple in design. Like *Deep Rover*, though, *Deep Flight* could only go about 3,000 feet (914 meters) deep.

By the end of the 1980s, Sylvia had accomplished a lot. She had started a new company and successfully completed two new ocean submersibles. She was also beginning to publish a lot of her work in journals and magazines. The 1980s, like so much of Sylvia's life, had been full of adventure and passion for her career.

7

Swimming with Recognition

By the 1990s, Sylvia's deter-
mination and hard work had gained
her the respect of scientists, the public,
and the government. She was considered
one of the best in her field, a great ocean
explorer much like William Beebe and Jacques
Cousteau. Her knowledge of the sea was pro-
found and phenomenal. Few others had even
attempted the adventurous exploration that Sylvia
had accomplished.

HEADING A NEW ADMINISTRATION

In 1990, President George H. W. Bush asked
Sylvia to head the National Oceanic
Atmospheric Administration (NOAA).

Sylvia, always up for a challenge, accepted the position with high hopes. She moved her family to Washington, D.C., and she plunged into her new job.

The goal of NOAA is to study human behavior in relation to the oceans. This meant Sylvia's job was to figure out how to help humans and fish lead a more peaceful and healthy coexistence. At the time, the fish population was being depleted at an alarming rate, and it was upsetting the balance of nature. Sylvia found herself flying to Japan and Iceland to speak with these countries' leaders about these pressing matters. The more she learned, the more worried she became. Sylvia cared deeply for oceans and they were being destroyed at a rapid rate.

Sylvia served the NOAA until her resignation in February 1992. She had a new goal to follow and wanted to focus all her energy on it.

OCEAN ACTIVIST

In the 1970s, when the Tektite project had ended, Sylvia had been launched into the public eye by public demand, but not by choice. In the 1990s, Sylvia reentered the mainstream media with one goal in mind: She wanted to educate the public about oceans and help keep them healthy and safe. She appeared on *Good Morning America* in 1994, 1996, 1997, and 2001. She was also featured on other TV shows to rally support for her cause. She wrote books that explained the fragile state of the oceans, including a series of children's books about fish and her own dives with the help of *National Geographic*. Sylvia wanted to make a difference.

STATE OF THE SEA

One of Sylvia's biggest concerns about the sea (and one of the reasons she became an ocean activist) was how polluted the sea had become. Many times on television, Sylvia shared how the amount of litter had increased during her dives—steadily, through the 1960s. She often spoke of her experiences in some of the most remote places, where she would see plastic netting attached to coral reefs. Many ocean dwellers are affected by the tons of trash being dumped into the ocean each year. Each piece of pollution takes away from the ocean's natural balance and usually creates a loss of marine life.

The Shinkai 6500 *is a Japanese vessel built to travel to depths as far as 13,065 feet (3,982 meters) deep. Sylvia gladly took the plunge in this submersible in 1992 and discovered again why she had fallen in love with the ocean.*

SHINKAI 6500

In 1992, while Sylvia was beginning her crusade to rid the oceans of pollution, she was offered a chance to go 13,065 feet (about 3,982 meters) deep. Diving at that depth was almost unbelievable to Sylvia—the deepest she had ever been was 3,300 feet (1,006 meters). She could not imagine what the ocean would be like so far down. Sylvia, always ready for a challenge, packed her bags and headed to Japan where she would meet the new, amazing *Shinkai 6500*.

The *Shinkai 6500* was a stunning accomplishment for Japan. The vessel went deeper and faster and glided more smoothly than any other submersible in the world. Sylvia was astounded at how comfortable her ride down was. The pilot even asked her if she wanted to listen to a CD!

It took Sylvia an hour and a half to go down two-and-a-half miles (about four kilometers). This was the quickest ride she could imagine. The *Shinkai 6500* cruised around as Sylvia caught sight of blazing blue jellyfish and other glowing creatures. The whole experience made her realize again just how vast and amazing the ocean was. When she returned to the surface, her activism had an even deeper tie. She felt even more passionate and determined to help her oceans. Only a few years later, she saw magnificent results.

YEAR OF THE OCEANS

While President Bill Clinton was in office, he made 1998 the "Year of the Oceans." He raised government funding for research projects and environmental awareness. Consequently, this brought oceanic life back into the spotlight. Scientists were enthused, but more important, people were learning about the deep blue sea, getting excited about the oceans, and starting to care about their future.

Former president Bill Clinton gives a thumbs-up for ocean conservation, as Sylvia (second from right) *looks on.*

HERO FOR THE PLANET

In 1998, *Time* magazine awarded Sylvia with an amazing achievement. She was named *Time*'s Hero for the Planet. Roger Rosenblatt's article, "Call of the Sea," described Sylvia in great detail: "She is a small-boned, fearless woman with a kid's keen face, deep brown eyes set far apart, and a jaw of character, like the young Katharine Hepburn's. Sometimes the alertness in her eyes and the quick, broad smile are disconnected."

Sylvia was excited about the award, and she knew she deserved it. She had given the world great knowledge of the sea. But she was also humble about it, because she never sought fame or recognition for her adventures. Each exploration was just simply another chance to learn about the sea, the place she loved best of all.

A LIFE OF SEA EXPLORATION

These days, Sylvia concentrates most on sharing her experiences with the world. She gives presentations at luncheons and speeches at universities,

Sylvia Earle has dedicated her life to exploring, research-
ing, and helping to preserve the oceans. Her activism has
paved the way for a deeper understanding of the ocean,
the creatures that call it home, and the need to keep it
clean and safe.

and she continues to be an ocean activist. She loves talking about the ocean and she still dives quite often. She will never lose her love for the sea—it is a part of her. These days when Sylvia takes the stage or gives an interview, she has a voice that everyone listens to. No one calls her a "girl" anymore; Sylvia Earle is proud to be a woman scientist.

From the Indian Ocean to the Galapagos Islands and back, Sylvia has just *seen*. She has witnessed the ocean's most astonishing elements and works hard to see more. Amazingly, she has gone 33,000 feet (about 10 kilometers) deep and returned just as wide-eyed and awed by the ocean as when she was three years old. She built her life around the waves, around the deep, around the bodies of water that still hold incredible mystery. Sylvia's work has brought scientists closer to understanding how we must take care of our oceans and how to keep this important water clean. She has never fallen out of love with the sea.

Sylvia has lived a true scientist's life. Her adventures and explorations have taken her to some of the most fascinating parts of the world, the world beneath. Her passion for her work is extraordinary and thought provoking. She challenges individuals to look out at the world the same way she does. She challenges everyone to see the unknown adventures everywhere.

TIMELINE

1935 On August 30, Sylvia Alice Earle is born in Gibbstown, New Jersey, to Lewis and Alice Earle.

1938 Young Sylvia and her family move to Paulsboro, New Jersey, to live on a farm. The farm's pond inspires Sylvia's first scientific investigations.

1951 Sylvia experiences her first breathing-assisted dive in the Weeki Wachee River in Florida.

1952 At seventeen years old, before graduating from high school, Sylvia enrolls in a marine biology class at Florida State University. There she meets Harold Humm, her first professor and a lifelong friend.

1955 Sylvia earns her bachelor's degree in marine botany from Florida State. She decidess to continue her education by pursuing a master's degree at Duke University.

1956 Sylvia earns her master's degree in marine botany from Duke University.

1964 Sylvia accepts a trip to travel all over the Indian Ocean aboard the *Anton Bruun*. This is her first scientific exploration into foreign waters.

1965 Sylvia discovers a new type of algae in the Mas a Tierra, a group of islands near Chile. She names the algae *Hummbrella hydra*, after her lifelong friend Harold Humm.

1968 Sylvia participates in an exploration called the Man-in-the-Sea Project. She dives from a small submarine called the *Deep Diver*. At this time, she's pregnant with her daughter Gale.

1970 Sylvia heads an all-female team of scientists on the Tektite Project, in which she and four other women scientists live in the ocean for two weeks.

1979 On October 19, Sylvia tests out the Jim suit and dives 1,250 feet (381 meters) into the ocean. She breaks the record for the deepest untethered dive in history.

1984 Sylvia's company, Deep Ocean Technology, meets with huge success when it unveils *Deep Rover*, a fantastic new underwater submersible.

1990 President Bush asks Sylvia to head the National Oceanic Atmospheric Administration (NOAA).

1992 Sylvia goes 13,065 feet (3,982 meters) deep in a Japanese watercraft called the *Shinkai 6500*.

1998 Sylvia is named *Time* magazine's first Hero for the Planet.

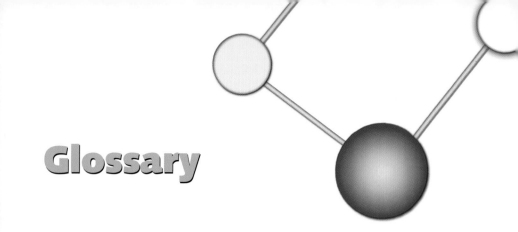

Glossary

advocate A person who talks to the public about the importance of a specific subject, trying to raise awareness, motivation, and support.

aquanaut A term used for divers who visit the ocean, much as astronauts visit space.

bends An illness that occurs when a diver's blood receives too much nitrogen; also called decompression sickness.

cultivate The act of helping to inspire growth or an interest in something.

decompression chamber A chamber used to reduce the pressure within a diver's body by changing oxygen and nitrogen levels.

ecology The study of the relationship between plants and animals and their environment.

ichthyology A branch of zoology that involves the study of fish.

marine botanist A person who studies the plant and animal life in a specific area; looks for what kind of plants live in the ocean, why they are important to the environment, fish, and other ocean animals.

nomenclature A system used in biology to classify different kinds and groups of animals and plants.

role model A person someone looks up to for his or her values, accomplishments, and the way he or she lives life.

specimen An item used for research and testing in experiments.

submersible A vessel used for underwater exploration, much like a very small submarine.

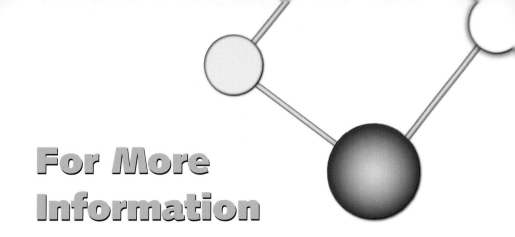

For More Information

The Coral Reef Alliance
2014 Shattuck Avenue
Berkeley, CA 94704-1117
(888) CORAL-REEF (267-2573)
e-mail: info@coral.org
Web site: http://www.coral.org

**National Oceanic and Atmospheric
 Administration (NOAA)**
14th Street & Constitution Avenue NW, Room 6013
Washington, DC 20230
(202) 482-6090
Web site: http://www.noaa.gov

Oceana
2501 M Street NW, Suite 300
Washington, DC 20037-1311
(877) 7-OCEANA (762-3262)

e-mail: info@oceana.org

Web site: http://www.oceana.org

The Ocean Conservancy

1725 DeSales Street, Suite 600

Washington, DC 20036

(202) 429-5609

e-mail: info@oceanconservancy.org

Web site: http://www.cmc-ocean.org

IN CANADA

Greenpeace Canada

250 Dundas Street West, Suite 605

Toronto, ON M5T 2Z5

(800) 320-7183

Web site: http://www.greenpeace.ca

Oceans Canada

Fisheries and Oceans Canada

Station 10N191

200 Kent Street

Ottawa, ON K1A 0E6

e-mail: oceanscanada@dfo-mpo.gc.ca

Web site: http://www.oceanscanada.com

WEB SITES

Due to the changing nature of Internet links, the Rosen Publishing Group, Inc., has developed an online list of Web sites related to the subject of this book. This site is updated regularly. Please use this link to access the list:

http://www.rosenlinks.com/whfsm/sear/

For Further Reading

Baker, Beth. *Sylvia Earle: Guardian of the Sea*. Minneapolis, MN: Lerner Publishing Group, 2000.

Earle, Sylvia A. *Dive: My Adventures in the Deep Frontier*. Washington, D.C.: National Geographic Society, 1999.

Earle, Sylvia A. *Wild Ocean: America's Parks Under the Sea*. Washington, D.C.: National Geographic Society, 1999.

Earle, Sylvia A., and Joelle Delbourgo. *Sea Change: A Message of the Oceans*. New York: Fawcett Books, 1995.

Earle , Sylvia A., and Eric Lindstrom. *Atlas of the Ocean: The Deep Frontier*. Washington, D.C.: National Geographic Society, 2001.

Powell, David C. *A Fascination for Fish: Adventures of an Underwater Pioneer*. Berkeley, CA: University of California Press, 2001.

Tucker, Lisa. *Meet My Grandmother: She's a Deep-Sea Explorer*. Brookfield, CT: Millbrook Press, 2000.

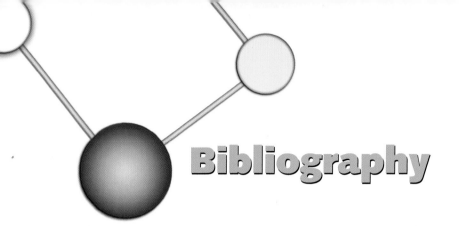

Bibliography

Baker, Beth. *Sylvia Earle: Guardian of the Sea.*
Minneapolis, MN: Lerner Publishing Group, 2000.

Earle, Sylvia A. *Sea Change: A Message of the Oceans.*
New York: Fawcett Books, 1995.

Gradwohl, Judith. Smithsonian Institution. "Ocean
Planet: Oceanic Facts." Retrieved March 20, 2002
(http://seawifs.gsfc.nasa.gov/OCEAN_PLANET/
HTML/education_oceanographic_facts.html).

Lawrence, Martin. Mount Sinai Hospital. "Scuba
Diving Explained: Questions and Answers on
Physiology and Medical Aspects of Scuba Diving."
Retrieved April 1, 2002 (http://www.mtsinai.org/
pulmonary/books/scuba/sectiong.htm).

Leff, Mark, and the Associated Press. CNN. "Jacques
Cousteau Remembered for His Common Touch."

June 25,1997. Retrieved March 25, 2002
(http://www.cnn.com/WORLD/9706/25/
cousteau.obit/index.html).

McDonald, Kendall. *Diver*. "A Visit from Aquababe
Number One." 1996. Retrieved January 25, 2002
(http://www.divernet.com/profs/earl1196.htm).

National Geographic Explorer. "Where Does
Oceanographer Sylvia Surf the Web?" Retrieved
February 26, 2002
(http://www.nationalgeographic.com/
bookmarks/earle).

Riverdeep Interactive Learning Limited. "Saving an
Underwater World." Retrieved January 25, 2002
(http://www.riverdeep.net/current/2001/01/
010201_sylvia.jhtml).

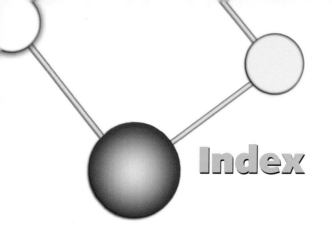

Index

SYLVIA EARLE

ABOUT THE AUTHOR

Katherine White is a freelance editor and writer. She lives in Jersey City, New Jersey.

DESIGN AND LAYOUT

Evelyn Horovicz

SERIES EDITOR

Eliza Berkowitz